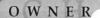

The Church That Works

Democracy vs. Theocracy

How giving back His church releases followers of Jesus Christ to serve and unleashes God's power to back them.

Rick DuBose
and Mel Surface

The Church That Works
Copyright © 2009 by Rick DuBose and Mel Surface

Printed in the United States of America
ISBN: 978-1-61658-375-0

To the deacons and other faithful men and women
of God who have helped us to discover
the blessings of being
a church that works.

Contents

Introduction

Growing up in a pastor's home brought me an early schooling in local church government and ministries. So much so that, for a time, I hid from God's call to preach. When my father asked if I had considered whether God might be calling me into fulltime ministry, I answered, "No, I will be the best deacon a pastor ever had, but I want to be a businessman."

Dad is an outstanding man of God and he was a great pastor, confirmed by growth and development of a dynamic church under his leadership and his subsequent election to top posts in our denomination. Still, I observed times of tension in the church.

Though he did not discuss it, more than once evidence suggested conflict. When he felt strongly about the direction the Lord wanted to take the church or simply what wisdom would dictate as a good decision, rather than a flow of support to get it done, opposition surfaced.

So, I said I did not want to go into the ministry. I believed the greater need was to become a good deacon to support what God says to the pastors. By my early 20s, God had made clear His will for my life and I surrendered to His call. Until then, I had struggled because I had seen the breakdown of God-given leadership.

After a series of volunteer and staff positions, and after the first steps of a ministry credentialing process, I was appointed pastor of a small congregation functioning under district oversight. In our fellowship, churches large enough and considered strong enough to be healthy are set in order as sovereign congregations.

Though the church began to grow, I was afraid to move from dependent to sovereign assembly because I knew I would have to have and face deacons. Consequently, I spent a lot of time training candidates and church members in biblical order before we took that step.

When issues did arise under the new order, when someone else wanted to take charge, I knew the responsibility was mine. I knew full well I did not have all the answers, but I also knew I was called to lead the flock. That forced me to go deeper in exploring the biblical flow of authority and pursuing the New Testament model for ministry.

By the time I moved to my next pastorate, another district affiliated assembly, I had worked carefully through the process. I took a lot of time training the new church in what I had learned.

As the church assumed sovereignty, the deacons and I had a clear understanding that we were there to find the will of God. They worked with me. I would teach a principle and we would work it out together. They would listen then vent back to me based upon what they had been told or what they had assumed a deacon's job to be.

We did all this with great friendship and, in a very practical way, we lived out a healthy pastor, healthy board, and healthy church process for the next 18 years. We developed the basic concepts of what we later called "democracy vs. theocracy," and we determined we wanted to be a powerful theocratic church.

Growing from an attendance of 17 to more than 800, Sachse Assembly of God became a strong influence for Christ in the community and a national leader in giving to world ministries. Moreover, the momentum continues. The church is multiplying outreaches and Sunday attendance has climbed to more than 2000 in the past four years under new Pastor Bryan Jarrett.

God poured out His Spirit Sunday after Sunday, and we watched and worked with Him as He developed leaders, workers, worshipers, and ministers. In fact, Sachse Assembly became a church full of ministers—individual believers doing relevant works of service.

Elected assistant superintendent for the North Texas District of the Assemblies of God in 2005 and district superintendent in 2007, I brought this lifetime focus on church health with me into denominational office. I discovered very quickly we have a lot of unhealthy churches. They are not positively impacting their communities, not winning people to Christ, and not living up to their potential. Sometimes, they not only sit stagnant but they have become a detriment to Christian witness.

Many factors may contribute to the problems, but one scenario plays out so frequently that we cannot ignore it. We often find a zealous but very frustrated pastor. Though he may need help with a detailed strategy, he wants the church to make a positive impact for God, but he is stymied by a democratic system which, in effect, has become an entrenched dictatorship.

Seeing this again and again, I became convinced that God had brought me through my own processes in order to position me to help pastors and churches facing these struggles. A series of 21 leadership banquets focusing on "Democracy vs. Theocracy" was the first step. This book is an extension of those banquet presentations.

Challenged to put the concepts into print, I needed a wordsmith who also burns with passion for healthy churches and Christ's Great Commission. I believe God brought Mel Surface to the close of a fifteen-year tenure as head of Discipleship and Adult Ministries for the North Texas District of the Assemblies of God, at least in part, to help deliver this message. Serving as a missionary, evangelist, church planter, pastor, and both national and district staff member gives Mel a reservoir of experience and a unique perspective for the task.

The Church that Works is not a comprehensive theological treatise. We do not pretend to exhaust the meaning and applications of the Scriptures cited. Neither is it a leadership manual. *The Church that Works* is a presentation of practical biblical principles and patterns for a healthy local church.

We are praying that pastors, leaders, and individual believers will grasp the power and process of a biblically ordered congregation. We pray this book will help motivate them to do whatever it takes to be that kind of church. Finally, we are praying for you that you will find in each chapter hope and real help to be *The Church That Works!*

Rick DuBose

Chapter 1

Whose Church Is It?

"We want our church back!"

A complainant in a local church lawsuit confronted the denominational officer with what he thought was a simple request. Actually, it was the root of the problem.

Confusion about who owns the church and who should be in charge is crippling American Christianity. Many congregations have reached growth plateaus, and many have begun decline, largely because their democratic approach to doing church stifles their impact. It can sidetrack the church from its eternal purpose and, consequently, choke the flow of God's power for relevant ministries.

How may we turn our churches right-side-up and put the people, not just the pastor, into the ministry? The key is recognizing Christ as the Owner and Head of the Church, embracing the biblical flow of authority through His ministry office gifts, and putting into practice the priesthood of believers.

Pentecostals and Evangelicals vigorously contend that Jesus Christ is Head of the Church, and that He established leadership offices for "equipping of the saints for the work of service."[1] We argue that every New Testament believer is a priest, but how we do church undermines what we say we believe.

We say we believe Christ is Head, but we jockey for power positions. We trust him with Eternity but we want to be in charge until we get there. We say we believe in equipping the saints for ministry, but we relate the bulk of the work to paid professionals. We believe Christ's death opened the way for us all to call on God, but we rely mostly on the preacher for prayer and intercession.

Becoming a healthy church means getting back to God's pattern. As we explore roles of pastors and deacons and the relationship between pastors and boards, we will discover that the New Testament process releases all the people of the church into relevant ministry. It also unleashes God's power to enable and confirm their efforts.

In many instances, good men and women fail to flow in God's purpose because they simply do not know their roles in God's process. These are the individuals most excited about the liberating truths in *The Church that Works*.

Night after night in a series of leadership banquets on "Democracy vs. Theocracy," local church board members responded: "We didn't know, and it's the only way we have seen church done. Now we see the Scriptures, and we realize this is NOT how to do it. We are going to change."

In a small assembly the first Sunday following one of the banquets, the deacons unnerved their young pastor when they gathered around and asked for a corner conference. They said, "We're going to take you to lunch today, and we will pay!"

Over the meal, they told him what was on their minds. They had evaluated their attitudes and overall approach to serving on the church board. They said they had been out of order and concluded with, "We're sorry and we are going to do better." They have kept their promise, and the pastor reports an incredible and continuing transformation in the life and ministries of the church.

So many local church board members responded this way that it became an expected part of each banquet evening. These were not arrogant or angry leaders. They were rightly motivated individuals who had been doing what they thought was their job, keeping the pastor accountable. They bubbled with relief to discover they are not divinely assigned to ride herd on the man of God. "Thank God! I can be what God called ME to be!"

It's His Church!
Authority Belongs to Christ

Whoever owns something has authority over it, and whoever pays for it owns it. Jesus Christ paid for the Church with His own blood and body. It is his Church and all the authority belongs to Him.

In Matthew 28:18, Jesus is about to ascend to His Father. He has been crucified and raised from the dead. As He addresses a large post-Resurrection crowd outside Jerusalem, He makes a definitive proclamation, "All authority in heaven and on earth has been given to me."

How much of it? All of it! It all belongs to Jesus. In Heaven, all the authority is His. He can say anything He wants, and the seraphim, cherubim, and all the angels hop to it. "And on earth…" He didn't just say in the Church. He said all authority on earth. He can stop the swirl of human events anytime He wants. He can interrupt and intervene. He still has all power and authority. (That is why we should sleep well at night. No matter what is going on, He still is in control!). We can be sure, then, all the authority in the Church belongs to Him.

Jesus said "I will build MY church", very possessive, "MY church".[2] It is His Church in ownership and authority. It is "our church" in the sense of membership, fellowship, privilege, and responsibility for service and support, but it is always HIS church.

When we begin to think it is OUR church and act as if it were "built for me"—we have issues. He bought it and He is building it according to His purpose. This is the first thing we must resolve. All the authority in the Church and in each local church belongs to Christ.

It's Your Church!
Ministry Belongs to the People

Every born-again believer should be in ministry inside and outside the meeting place. Putting the ministry into the office of the pastor alone robs the church of power and denies the community the help it desperately needs.

The term "ministry" today typically refers to a career pursuit of preaching, teaching, worship leading, and other duties of religious professionals. The verb "minister" most often applies to the efforts of a pastor, teacher, singer, or musician. The New Testament, while it includes all of these, shows a much richer meaning.

Ministry is God's love reaching people through the infinite variety of gifts He has given to His children. He gives every one of us the ability to do something well and the responsibility to do it.

The Apostle Paul addressed these gifts and responsibilities in his letter to the Romans:

> *Just as each of us has one body with many members, and these members do not all have the same function, so in Christ we who are many form one body, and each member belongs to all the others. We have different gifts, according to the grace given us. If a man's gift is prophesying, let him use it in proportion to his faith. If it is serving, let him serve; if it is teaching, let him teach; if it is encouraging, let him encourage; if it is contributing to the needs of others, let him give generously; if it is leadership, let him govern diligently; if it is showing mercy, let him do it cheerfully.*[3]

He emphasized the truth again to the church at Corinth in his discourse on spiritual gifts:

> *There are different kinds of gifts, but the same Spirit. There are different kinds of service, but the same Lord. There are different kinds of working, but the same God works all of them in all men.*[4]

In the Greek of the New Testament, Paul uses a form of the same word for "serving" and "serve" in Romans 12:7 as for "service" in 1 Corinthians 12:5. The words derive from the noun *diakonos*, for "attendant" or "servant" (and the verb *diakoneo* for "minister" or "serve").

It is the same term which the writer Luke applies variously in Acts 6:1-4 to serving in distribution of food and attending tables, as well as to preaching and teaching the Word of God. Ministry is any service which brings God's love to bear on human needs. Whenever you receive the Lord Jesus Christ as Savior, you become His servant. You enter the ministry.

The Samaritan woman at the well in John 4 is a good example. Jesus connects with her in conversation, diverts her efforts to argue religion, and identifies her specific needs. She begins to understand when she refers to the prophesied Messiah, or Christ, and Jesus replies, "I who speak to you am he."[5]

She left her water pot and rushed into town to tell everyone she could, "Come, see a man who told me everything I ever did. Could this be the Christ?"[6]

Many people from the town came and believed in Him because of the woman's testimony, and many more believed after hearing Him for themselves.

She had been a believer only minutes, but she started telling others about Jesus. If we are not careful, we make ministry something far off and limited to special people. We prescribe classes and on-line studies and make it hard for people to go to work for God. Jesus didn't. The moment you become a Christian, you can begin.

You may be thinking, "I don't have any skills," but that is not the issue. When Peter attempted to divert Jesus' questions about his commitment to a question about John, the Lord said, "...what is that to you? You must follow me."[7]

What others may do or whether someone else might do a given task better has no bearing on God's call for you to serve Him. It is a cliché but still true... the first ability many tasks require is avail-ability. Are you willing?

The four men in Mark 2:3 carried their paralyzed friend to Jesus. So many people were crowding into the building that they could not get their friend through the door. So, they ripped a hole in the roof and lowered him in front of the Master.

The Gospel writer says, "When Jesus saw their faith,"[8] He forgave the man's sins and healed him. Faith? All they did was tear off the roof, but they did it to position a friend to receive from God. They were not builders that day, just a demolition team, but they did it in faith and love, and miracles resulted.

Some speculate it was Peter's house where this took place and where Jesus had healed his mother-in-law. Peter may have been thinking about his time, "Lord, you've got to find another place to do your work."

Certainly, you can grow and develop in ministry, and you should, but you do not have to wait to get started. The church is on the right track when the pastor and the people understand that we all are priests, we all can be filled with the Holy Spirit, and we all have ministry. All authority belongs to Jesus, but the ministry belongs to the church.

The Apostle Peter taught that all Christians are priests to God.

You also, like living stones, are being built into a spiritual house to be a holy priesthood, offering spiritual sacrifices acceptable to God through Jesus Christ. For in Scripture it says: "See, I lay a stone in Zion, a chosen and precious cornerstone, and the one who trusts in him will never be put to shame." Now to you who believe, this stone is precious. But to those who do not believe, "The stone the builders rejected has become the capstone," and, "A stone that causes men to stumble and a rock that makes them fall." They stumble because they disobey the message — which is also what they were destined for. But you are a chosen people, a royal priesthood, a holy nation, a people belonging to God, that you may declare the praises of him who called you out of darkness into his wonderful light.[9]

The priesthood was central to God's plan in the Old Testament. Under the Law, an individual seeking God would bring an offering, whatever the Law prescribed, to the house of God, the tabernacle or, later, the Temple and give it to the priest.

The priest would present it to the Lord in behalf of the suppliant, and God would receive it. If anyone else attempted to present the offering, God would not accept it. Only a priest was ordained for that service, and only the High Priest could enter the Most Holy Place once a year with a blood sacrifice to intercede for the whole nation.

This was the process God had put into place. Going the other way, the priest was God's representative to the people. He spoke and taught His laws and precepts through the priest. The priest was the intermediary, representing the people to God and God to the people.

Then comes the New Testament, as if Jesus says, "Through My blood, through salvation, and through birth into this Kingdom, all of you now are priests." Everyone is a priest, which means we each can go directly to God. You don't have to get on the phone and say, "Pastor, I need you to pray because I need God to help me..." Certainly, you can call and he or she will be eager to help, but you also have direct access to the Father. God has cut out the earthly middle man.

As a believer in Jesus Christ, the one Mediator between God and men, you can call anytime with confidence that He hears, cares, and will respond. You have the constant relationship of a priest, and you are in the ministry

Chapter 2

What Is The Church That Works?

"The Church that Works" is an ambitious title, but it captures a vital two-fold emphasis. First, it means a local body of Christian believers effectively representing their Lord and pursuing His commission to reach their world. Second, that church necessarily will be one in which the people, not just the clergy, do the work of ministry.

The word "church" today carries a variety of meanings. It can refer to a building used for public worship, to the congregation that assembles, to the public worship that takes place, to the activities or functions carried out by or in behalf of the congregation, or to a group of churches joined in doctrine and organization as a religious denomination.

Usage has mutated since the First Century when the Greek word translated "church" throughout the New Testament, e*kklesia,* referred to an assembly or congregation. Specifically, it meant a meeting or body of people called out by a herald representing some civil authority. The inspired writers adapted and applied it to the Christian congregation.

In Acts, *ekklesia* is the most frequent designation for the community of disciples. It denotes the body of Christians in a specific city or region such as Jerusalem (Acts 5:11; 8:1,

Antioch (Acts 11:26), and Caesarea (Acts 18:22). It also applies to the believers in all the churches (Acts 9:31).

For the purposes of this book, we use the word "church" to mean a local assembly of believers and the capitalized "Church" to refer to all those of all the world and of all times whom Christ has redeemed.

The New Testament makes clear that the Church Universal, the spiritual family of God including all followers of Christ, is visible and expressed in local bodies of believers—local churches who are functioning in cooperative fellowship. Everything the Universal Church represents, the local church embodies at a specific address.

Every local church should be healthy. It should faithfully present and practice the teachings of the Bible as God's Word. It should devote its fullest efforts and resources to carrying the good news of Jesus Christ to everyone everywhere. It should worship God in spirit and in truth, and the healthy local church must be building believers who live, love, and serve in the likeness of Christ.

A healthy church is marked by unity, cooperation, and mutual submission of its members for the sake of Christ and His mission. The pastor leads and gives priority to preparing and releasing all the believers to do the work of ministry according to their gifts. In every sense, the healthy church is a church that works.

The church that works keeps its own children, reaches its neighbors, blesses its community, and makes God known to its generation, and the next, around the world. More than a building and more than just a congregation of worshipers, the church is a body of Christian workers.

When the church works, the world wins. When the church works, people come to Christ. When the church works, lives are changed and families are transformed.

The New Testament church is a church that works. The people, not just the pastor, pray. The members, not just the ministerial staff, visit and serve the needy. Each believer, not just the paid worker or ministry leader, gives a witness for Christ in attitude and action.

Churches in the New Testament worked. They filled the city of Jerusalem with the teachings of Jesus Christ, then "turned the world upside down"[10] with dynamic demonstration of their faith.

The church worked then because each person who came to faith in Christ took responsibility for passing it along. The church worked because leaders recognized their divine assignment to equip the people to serve God and others.

The church worked because the leaders were free to pursue their tasks with the backing of the members. Finally, the church worked because pastors and members all relied on the empowering presence of the Holy Spirit.

When the people falter in ministry, the church fails in its mission. The church cannot work if the people who are called to lead are forced to follow or if those called to follow are trying to lead.

Christ paid for the Church with His own blood when He died on the Cross. He poured out His Spirit on the Church to energize us for service. He placed offices, and He calls officers, in His Church to channel His authority and keep us on target.

For the church to work, we must do it God's way. When we move away from His pattern and purpose, for whatever reason, we forfeit His power and provision. When we do the work for which we were called and authority flows the way God designed, the church will work.

Chapter 3

Christ Channels His Authority
Ministry Offices—*Apostles*

As Owner and Head of the Church, Christ chooses whom He will send in His name and authority. He establishes leadership positions and He determines who will fill them. The Apostle Paul's Letter to the Ephesians gives a pattern.

But to each one of us grace has been given as Christ apportioned it. This is why it says: "When he ascended on high, he led captives in his train and gave gifts to men." (What does "he ascended" mean except that he also descended to the lower, earthly regions? He who descended is the very one who ascended higher than all the heavens, in order to fill the whole universe.) It was he who gave some to be apostles, some to be prophets, some to be evangelists, and some to be pastors and teachers, to prepare God's people for works of service, so that the body of Christ may be built up until we all reach unity in the faith and in the knowledge of the Son of God and become mature, attaining to the whole measure of the fullness of Christ. [11]

Isaiah 9:6 says about the Messiah, "The government will be on his shoulders." This will be fulfilled in Christ's coming Kingdom, but it should be true now in His Church. He determines how the government functions, how authority is distributed.

Ephesians 4:7-13 is the distribution list. It is not just about ministry gifts and responsibilities, though these are very responsible positions and the officers are gifts to the church. It also has to do with authority. God never gives responsibility without the authority to fulfill it.

For example, He told Adam and Eve in the beginning to populate the earth. With the command, He gave them the ability to procreate and authority over His creation. He never sends you to do something without empowering you to do it.

God releases different authority to each ministry office in order to fulfill specific responsibilities in the Church. Office holders walk in submission to Him but also work in His authority. They are to put all the people into ministry so the body of Christ will be built, unity will grow, and believers will mature to be more and more like Jesus. Under this flow, every one of us will have the appropriate authority—pastors to lead, deacons to support and assist, and believers to minister.

Paul's list in Ephesians begins with "apostles." The word in the Greek text means "sent one." Many believe the office of apostle was limited to the 12 identified in the Gospels and Acts and to Paul who saw the Lord Jesus and received their teaching directly from Him.[12] Certainly, these Apostles, eyewitnesses of the resurrected Christ and Holy Spirit inspired authors of the New Testament, have no successors in any age. However, they also provided oversight and accountability for ministers and churches which God has ordained for every generation. Others in Acts also are identified as individuals sent from God, apostles, to lead and serve his church.

Some believe the term "apostle" best applies today to missionaries because they are sent to where Christ is not known. God calls missionaries and the churches send them. They are supported by and accountable to the churches. God does give them authority and He backs their ministry with supernatural power to bring down strongholds of darkness. Still, they do not fill a role of oversight for ministers and churches except, sometimes, in their specific fields of labor.

The Church that Works is not concerned with the office of an apostle but with oversight and accountability for churches and ministers. Our purpose is to explore the flow of divine authority which releases and empowers individual believers to work for God. We cannot detail here the exciting aspects of the term "apostolic" which relate to supernatural expressions of God's power to confirm and advance the message of Jesus Christ. However, getting the church right in authority sets the stage for God to do wonderful things.

In the New Testament church, and in Paul's list, "apostle" implies "sent with authority"—sent *from* somebody, as much as *to* somebody. It means "sent from God," not just sent to the lost. Our English word is a transliteration of the Greek *apostolos*, derived from *apostellein*, which is "to send." *Apostellein* emphasizes commission, authority from, and responsibility to the sender. So, an apostle is one sent on a mission in which he acts with full authority on behalf of the sender and is accountable to him.[13]

When someone designates another person to act in his behalf, to speak in his name, he gives him or her an affidavit or some official authorization. He gives his representative authority. Then, though he may not physically be present, his agent can make sure his wishes are implemented. Since the emissary acts with his authority and speaks in his stead, the sender will back him with all of his resources.

This describes the apostle for the purpose of this book. He is sent from God, and for God, to accomplish things God wants done. He serves and leads in the authority the Lord has distributed to him.   Specifically, he gives oversight and a channel of accountability for pastors and churches.

In addition to the original 12, with Matthias replacing Judas the Traitor, and Paul as Apostle to the Gentiles, the New Testament recognizes other individuals as apostles. Galatians 1:19 refers to James, the Lord's brother and head of the Jerusalem church, as an apostle. First Corinthians 15:7 includes him and, possibly, others besides The Twelve as apostles.

Paul's sponsor into the Jerusalem fellowship, and later his coworker, Barnabus also is identified as an apostle in Acts 14:4 and again in verse 14. Paul's relatives Adronicus and Junias are noted among the apostles in Romans 16:7. Paul's associates Silvanus and Timothy and their rights to assert apostolic authority are cited in 1 Thessalonians 2:6. The New Testament writers recognized specific anointing, gifting, and authority in all these individuals as sent from God to the churches.

The Apostles, moved by the Holy Spirit, gave us the New Testament without spelling out the oversight details of the office as it relates to governing the churches. They appear to have weighed in to resolve doctrinal issues, as in Acts 15, and to confirm policies and procedures for the churches. After cataloguing external hardships and sacrifices for ministry, Paul says in 2 Corinthians 11:28, "Besides everything else, I face daily the pressure of my concern for all the churches."

Every pastor and congregation needs to function under some form of apostolic covering. This means someone outside the local church who is anointed and sent with authority from God to hold them accountable in ministry content and personal and congregational conduct.

This apostolic function for spiritual authority may take different forms. It may come by relationship, a spiritual father-child bond with an obviously anointed veteran pastor. Paul encouraged, admonished, and instructed Timothy and Titus each as a "true son" in the faith.[14] They were saved or spiritually nurtured under his ministry, and his letters to them reflect the tender but clear authority of a good dad.

Accountability and guidance also may come through other pastors, not necessarily immediate fathers in the faith, who demonstrate an apostolic anointing for leadership beyond the local church. The Holy Spirit can draw pastors and congregations into this kind of relationship.

The weakness of relational submission is that sin, stubbornness, or simple pride, may disrupt the link. In addition, even the best counsel becomes suspect if it is not tempered with multiple wise perspectives.

Denominations and various associations of churches provide for oversight in their constitutions, bylaws, credentialing processes, and organizational structures. Their executive officers, governing boards, or oversight committees can fulfill an apostolic accountability function.

An exciting spiritual dynamic is revealed as God moves into specific leadership positions those individuals whom He has called, anointed, and gifted. Many times it is obvious long before they officially take office—much like David in the Old Testament who carried a royal anointing for years before God sat him on the throne of Israel.

The churches are blessed dramatically when a person anointed for leadership is installed in the position. It can be disappointing, even detrimental, when individuals, even good men, without that anointing and gifting are posted in authority. When we vote, we should take care that spiritual prerequisites guide our ballots and not personalities or personal preferences.

Non-denominational congregations may covenant with other churches or ministers for a submission to biblical authority. New Life Church of Colorado Springs, Colorado is an example.[15] The church survived crisis and a fallen pastor began restoration because they had such an apostolic agreement in place.

Founder and Pastor Ted Haggard led the congregation 22 years from 14 people meeting in his garage to more than 14,000 members with multi-million dollar facilities and worldwide ministries. His confession of immorality and resignation from the pastorate in 2006 devastated the church and shocked the Evangelical world. However, the bylaws provision for external authority gave the church and the pastor a door to recovery. At the time of the controversy, a group of four pastors from outside the church, the Overseers, had authority to investigate allegations of misconduct by the senior pastor.

The agreement empowered them to discipline or remove the pastor. Since Haggard confessed his sins and resigned all positions, they were not required to intervene. However, he asked to continue in an accountability relationship with them.[16] In the case of New Life Church, the Overseers also must confirm selection of a new pastor.

Whether through an organizational affiliation or otherwise, every pastor and church must find a covering. Without it, no one can walk in the full flow of God's authority for any ministry. Even the Apostles submitted to authority. Peter took six men with him, twice the required number of witnesses, when he obeyed the Holy Spirit and shared the good news of Jesus in the house of the Roman Cornelius. The account appears in Acts 10 and 11. He returned to report to the Apostles and fellow believers.

Acts 15 gives details of the first church council where the Apostles and elders addressed the issue of whether non-Jewish believers also are required to keep the Law of Moses for salvation. Peter's experience and the missionary reports from Barnabus and Paul, backed by the written Word, carried the day. Gentiles and Jews, as well, are saved through faith in the Lord Jesus Christ alone.

This chapter in Acts demonstrates churches cooperating in council and submitting to the counsel of external leadership. Churches and pastors in cooperation with and submission to others will avoid much pain and confusion. Truly independent churches and pastors may have nowhere to go if they fall apart.

Their people end up running to stable churches or, tragically, dropping out altogether.

Chapter 4

Christ Channels His Authority
Prophets and Evangelists

The next gifts on Paul's list are prophets and evangelists. While they are not directly related to local church governance, God has vested both offices with authority vital to a healthy church.

More "forth-tellers" than "foretellers," prophets speak to the church with a specific message from God. They may be likened to spiritual policemen with an authority from God and ability to see things that are not right. They address those things with anointed clarity.

They speak specifically to establish a biblical standard. The Bible teaches us that when the enemy comes in like a flood, God will raise up a standard against him.

If flood waters surge through a town and the river keeps overflowing its banks, wisdom demands a levee. Someone will step forward with a plan to lift up a standard higher than the flood stage. The problem comes with new generations who, safe behind the dam, have never seen the death and devastation of waters raging over the countryside. They do not recognize the value of the standard.

They begin to chip away at the levee or call for its removal altogether. "That big pile of dirt is an obstacle, an eyesore, and a hindrance to what we want," they reason. "Let's take it down, put it in our flower beds and gardens. We will be more comfortable, the town will be more appealing, and everything will grow."

So, they dynamite the levee, and you know the rest. The enemy comes in like a flood. Then, they rush to fill the sand bags and improvise a dam. They try desperately to reestablish the levee as they remember or discover why another generation built the wall.

It is easy and common for new generations to throw off the standards of older generations without taking the time to ask, "Why did they do that?" The Bible cautions about removing the ancient boundary stone. It was put there for a reason.

The prophet comes, sees the church involved in things we never have considered an issue, and he calls us on it. He says, "Do you know why?" And he begins to put the stones back in place. He helps the church keep its standard set and its focus where it needs to be for spiritual health, safety, and fulfillment of its mission.

We still need prophets in the church. When the real prophet of God comes, he will keep us from dropping vital standards. Or, he may warn us to stop holding as sacred things which are irrelevant. If we turn away from the prophets because they make us uncomfortable, we will be even more uncomfortable later because we did not embrace this gift of Christ to His Church.

Evangelists come next in Paul's list. Their authority is not so much with the church as with the lost, those who do not know Christ as Savior. They have an incredible authority with lost people.

One of my former staff members is an evangelist. In other areas of the church, he might fumble and stumble, but with lost people, he comes to life. On a ministry conference trip with the church staff, we were stretching during a service station break when a carload of young people wheeled into the drive. Boisterous and loud, with tattoos, piercings and multi-colored hair in funky fashions, they were intimidating, even for a veteran pastor.

Not for our evangelist. He had come from that culture and was unfazed by their appearance. He is anointed to be an evangelist, so he said, "Pastor, I've got to go and talk to them," and something incredible began to unfold. He bent over, looked into the driver's window and opened a conversation. "Do you guys know you are going straight to Hell?" Now, I would have said something like, "Man, do you know that Jesus loves you a lot?" and tried to connect along that line.

My staff member, the evangelist, said, "I used to be just like you. I used to live just like you. I used to look just like you and I really thought that the things of this world were going to make me happy." They sat in shock but they listened, and, in just a few moments, those burly teens began to cry. He told them to get out of the car, and they said "Yes, sir, and what are we going to do?" He said, "Kneel down and repeat after me." They all began to pray, and they meant it!

These kids are coming to Christ in the open air, and I am still filling my gas tank and thinking, "Wasn't that the coolest thing?" The evangelist has an authority with lost people.

Next, he noticed a truck with an older gentleman waiting for his wife to go in and buy a drink. The man may have witnessed the impromptu prayer meeting. My associate ran over, put out his hand, and said "Hey sir, how are you doing?" Then, he began to tell about God and His power to change lives today. The man said, "I used to be a Christian," and when he was reminded he needed to get right with God, he said, "I know, I know." In just a moment, he was praying a sinner's prayer over the steering wheel.

No one in those church vans could have done that except the one called and anointed to be an evangelist. He has an authority with lost people and they don't run from him. They know.

Even in the church service, the evangelist's authority is with the non-believers. After one Sunday morning message, four or five individuals of the hundreds there for the second service came forward at my closing invitation. I thought that was pretty good. Four or five every week is pretty good. I was about to lead them in prayer when I sensed the Holy Spirit urging to me let the staff evangelist close.

I resisted, thinking I had done a good job, very pastoral, but I could not ignore the inner nudge. I stepped back and called him by name. When I looked at him, he said, "Thank you, Pastor." He had been about to explode under the evangelist's anointing. He stepped to the microphone and, it seemed to me, began to tear into the congregation.

I had been saying, "Jesus loves you so much and God wants to take all those sins away because they hurt you, destroy you, and some day they are going to take you to Hell. But He loves you so much that He died for you and wants you to come to Him."

The evangelist took a different approach. "You know you are a sinner! Don't sit out there and hide amongst the Christians and act like you think you are going to Heaven. You are not going to Heaven! You know you are not, and we know you are not and, yes sir, we know what you've been doing!" The next thing we knew, 20 people were coming forward.

We still need evangelists in the house of the Lord—not just out-of-work pastors trying to make a living on weekends— but men and women who have an authority with lost people. They are out there. God still is calling them and anointing them with His Spirit.

Evangelists will come into your church and get people saved. It will not be very long before they start drawing new people. It is incredible and people will keep on coming. You might say, "How is this happening?" and I really do not know, except it is God's doing. It is supernatural.

The evangelist has an authority with lost people and they get excited about this ministry office in a way different than they do the local pastor. We each need to pray, "God, give us an evangelist, one You have called and given authority to help us win the lost!"

Chapter 5

Christ Channels His Authority
Pastors-Teachers

Number four on Paul's ministry office list is "pastors and teachers." The Greek in this text for "pastors and teachers" seems to indicate two aspects of one office, the shepherd of the local church.

"Pastor" means "shepherd," the one who leads, feeds, and protects the flock. Here, it refers to the church shepherd, watching over the flock of God. Paul emphasized this responsibility in his last meeting with the elders from the church at Ephesus. He said:

> *Keep watch over yourselves and all the flock of which the Holy Spirit has made you overseers. Be shepherds of the church of God, which he bought with his own blood. I know that after I leave, savage wolves will come in among you and will not spare the flock.*[17]

The Apostle Peter delivered the same message in his general letter to the churches.

> *To the elders among you, I appeal as a fellow elder, a witness of Christ's sufferings and one who also will share in*

*the glory to be revealed: Be shepherds of God's flock that is
under your care, serving as overseers--not because you must,
but because you are willing, as God wants you to be; not
greedy for money, but eager to serve; not lording it over those
entrusted to you, but being examples to the flock. And when the
Chief Shepherd appears, you will receive the crown of glory
that will never fade away.* [18]

Overseeing the flock means protecting it. The shepherd
carries a staff, not just to prod the sheep, but to fend off wolves
and other predators. Jesus said it best, "No one can enter a
strong man's house and carry off his possessions unless he first
ties up the strong man. Then he can rob his house."[19] He was
talking about His power over Satan, but the principle is true in
any house.

A pastor is the strongman in the house of God. When he
is strong in the Lord, strong in truth and righteousness, and
strong in his anointing, the devil has a hard time disrupting the
church. The only way he can disrupt it is to bind up the pastor.
We should make certain he never can use us to do it! Don't
hand him the rope!

The pastor is the strongman as well for the church's health
and stability. He maintains order and discipline when the lambs
get too rambunctious butting heads.

He also walks among the sheep for comfort. He stays with
them through storms. His character and faithfulness soothe and
reassure. "It's going to be alright. I'm here and I represent the
King of Kings and the Lord of Lords. I stand not in my own
authority, but in the authority Jesus gave me to be shepherd of

this flock. In His authority, like David who took on the lion and the bear and prevailed, I can take on the devil. So, let's just stay here. It's going to be all right." The good shepherd helps bring peace to the church.

Through it all, the pastor leads the sheep to good pastures and fresh water. He pours food into their lives. He blesses them with growth as he studies the Word and passes it along to them. Why? So they can get into the ministry, bear lambs, and produce wool. The pastor-teacher leads and feeds the church so each member can be and do all that God intends.

The effective pastor understands that the ministry, the wonderful array of works and service which reveal and apply God's love, really does not belong to him. It belongs to the people. His ministry priority is to put them into the ministry.

Chapter 6

What about Deacons?

Deacons do not appear on the ministry office lists in Ephesians or First Corinthians. So, what are they, where did they come from, and what do they do?

The office of deacon rose out of the need to expand church ministries yet keep the called leadership focused on why God called them—to feed the sheep. Deacons were first selected to look after the needs of the poor and to free the apostles to give themselves to prayer, preaching, and teaching.

The account is given in Acts 6:1-6:

> *In those days when the number of disciples was increasing, the Grecian Jews among them complained against the Hebraic Jews because their widows were being overlooked in the daily distribution of food. So the Twelve gathered all the disciples together and said, "It would not be right for us to neglect the ministry of the word of God in order to wait on tables. Brothers, choose seven men from among you who are known to be full of the Spirit and wisdom. We will turn this responsibility over to them and will give our attention to prayer and the ministry of the word."*

This proposal pleased the whole group. They chose Stephen, a man full of faith and of the Holy Spirit; also Philip, Procorus, Nicanor, Timon, Parmenas, and Nicolas from Antioch, a convert to Judaism. They presented these men to the apostles, who prayed and laid their hands on them.

The Apostles asked the people to give them qualified men to whom they could give the responsibilities of food distribution. Then, they prayed and laid hands on them to commission them with the authority necessary to fulfill their tasks.

Deacons, from the Greek *diakonos* for "servant," were introduced to address a problem. Deacons address problems.
The Jerusalem church had mushroomed so that the daily administration and ministry operation required more people to get everything done. Someone needed to organize and oversee and someone had to do the work.

People had begun to complain because they thought they were not getting what was fair. This remains a common pattern in local churches. A shortage of workers, lack of administration, and poor ministry coordination will produce complaints.

The Apostles told the congregation they could not take over serving tables, the food distribution, because it would force them to neglect serving the Word of God. Getting caught up in the daily operations and handling complaints would keep them from feeding the sheep and putting each one of them into God-called service.

They called on the people to choose seven men from their ranks, respected and recognized as full of the Holy Spirit and wisdom, to whom they could commit these necessary duties.

"Full of the Spirit" describes a current condition in their relationship with God, not a past experience. The seven were to manifest the initial physical evidence of Baptism in the Spirit, speaking in other tongues, and the continuing evidence of power to be witnesses in word and deed. The fruit of the Spirit, the character traits of Christ Himself, were to flourish in their lives.

Later, Paul would tell the churches not to present a novice or new convert for this responsibility.[20] Smaller churches, especially, are tempted to rush people into leadership. They say something like, "Well, we have enough men for deacons now, Pastor. Ol' John got saved last week."

Paul instructed the churches not to lay hands hastily on anyone. That is, do not commission an unready candidate for service as a church leader. If you do not have truly qualified deacons, leave the spot open. Again, if God has not provided for the quality you need, leave the post vacant. If anyone questions, tell them, "We dare not do it any other way. It will save us all a lot of trouble."

Rushing a candidate prematurely into leadership diminishes the church and disserves the individual. The church misses the spiritual maturity and wisdom needed for essential tasks, and the individual may be injured, overwhelmed, and, even, corrupted by having to "wing it" in the face of high expectations and low expertise.

The Jerusalem disciples brought to the apostles seven qualified men. Prayer and laying on of hands by the Apostles, the original pastors of the Jerusalem church, recognized the divine channels of authority[21] in the church. The implication is, "The authority in the church is ours from the Lord, and we give it to you to operate in the ministry of servanthood. You have authority as delegated through the pastors."

Incredible things happened when the deacons began to serve. They straightened out the benevolence ministry, got involved in the daily administration, and restored unity to the church family. Meanwhile, the apostles continued praying and preaching and a new surge of revival multiplied the ranks of believers.

The pastor should not be mired in the details of the church operation.   Being God's businessman can consume him. Ultimately, it is the pastor's responsibility. He has to make sure it is happening, but, if he has to take care of it all, he will wear himself out. He will have little left to give on Sundays. Deacons should help carry the load.

Good deacons also help the pastor and serve the church by responding to complainers. Some people believe deacons exist so they will have somebody on whom to dump their criticism of the pastor. The unwary deacon often plays into their hands and becomes their advocate, "Pastor, Brother Jones is all upset and he wants you to…"

A better way to process complaints says, "Thank you for telling me that. It's my job to hear the complaints. Now, my first responsibility is to see whether or not there is any validity to your complaint."

Validity means substance. Are the issues real or is this merely a case of someone ruffled by not getting his or her way? When you say you will check it out, not infrequently, the plaintiff will downsize the issue with "It's really no big deal, now that I'm thinking about it."

If there is credibility, do not rush to the pastor with the report. Pray and think through the situation asking, "What can we do to fix this problem?"

By the time you get to the pastor, you can say, "We heard about some stuff going on and we checked it out. It's probably happening, and here's an idea for what we can do to fix it. *If you will give me the authority,* I'll take care of it for you. "

That is being a good deacon. That is an Acts 6 caliber deacon. Then the pastor can say, "Thanks for keeping me informed and keeping me free for prayer and study."

When deacons serve in the ongoing functions of the church and help to field complaints, they release the pastor to pray and prepare for his priority. They release him to feed the people.

When you really get it right, so that the pastor is feeding the people the way they need, they can mature. They will become so much more healthy and happy that you will have far fewer problems to confront. It all connects.

Deacons who submit and serve well in the church will have greater authority at home and elsewhere. They also will have more spiritual power and the hope of a great eternal reward. Paul instructed the young pastor Timothy, "Those who are deacons and do it well will receive a great reward."[22]

A Special Note for Deacons

Deacon, this suggests a wonderful scene at the Judgment Seat of Christ. Your pastor will be called up and the whole church will witness and wonder, "What reward will God give our pastor?"

Christ will say, "Pastor, you did well. You influenced your city and faithfully preached to the people. They matured and everywhere they went they preached the gospel because you poured life into them. You poured truth into them. You encouraged them, and, when they needed it, you scolded for their sakes. You are a great shepherd. You did an excellent job.

"Well done! I have a great reward for you, **but first, I'd like all your deacons to come stand with you.** You could not have done it had they not been faithful in what I called them to do. I am giving you the reward, and I am going to give to them the same reward because they enabled you to be all I called you to be."

Ultimately, that is what being a deacon is all about.

Chapter 7

Democracy vs. Theocracy

Here is what happens in many churches to short-circuit the biblical flow of authority. We concern ourselves more with democracy than with fulfilling our Christian purpose. Even though we know the Scripture says the government shall be upon His shoulders, we insist it belongs on the shoulders of the people.

Democracy is the best governing system in the world for nations but not for the local church. If the people have the authority, and that is how democracy works, then the people have the voice and the vote to decide what the church will be and do. The majority, not necessarily God, rules.

The people typically exercise control through their representatives. By contrast, God dispensed His authority in the New Testament through His appointed and called representatives. This is the theocracy discussed in upcoming chapters.

Since they elect representatives to rule in their behalf, it is easy for church people to extend the process. They think, "We've got all this church work that has to be done. Let's hire somebody." So, they employ, or elect, a pastor to do the work. Basically, they contract with someone and pay him to fill the position, which means he works for them. Jesus used the term "hireling" as a negative contrast to Himself as the true Shepherd. Hiring and firing preachers calls to mind His expression.

In this system, the authority Christ intended to flow through His ordained offices is transferred to the people. The majority elects deacons to govern and the pastor is left doing the majority of the ministry.

This takes the limitless ministry potential of Christ's church and bottlenecks it to one person, or to a pastoral staff. We funnel it to an individual and he has to make the hospital calls and visits to everyone who needs him to pray for them. The pastor is expected to go to each class, department, and individual member's party. He also should drop in on the wedding and baby showers. Then he has to return all the calls and messages that come in while he runs everywhere to pray and encourage people.

The pastor must spend his day and much of his night scurrying about in his duties. He wears himself out for the church and still has to show up at every community function. He represents the church. (If we all are the "church," it has representation everywhere, pastor or not!).

This scenario makes "the ministry" all about what the pastor does. He is worn out before Sunday comes. He feels down because he has no time to spend with the Lord in prayer and study. Oh, he has a little time by staying up late and getting up early, but he is so tired in the pulpit that even he has trouble staying awake.

Then somebody has the nerve to complain, "He just doesn't feed me anymore." Americans have a tragically me-focused snapshot of being a Christian when it is not about "me" at all. What would happen if we put it back into proper order? What would happen if we understood that the church never was meant to be a democracy and that the authority never was given to the people?

All authority belongs to Christ and He chooses whom He wills. It has to be His choice. In our way of doing business, we hire the pastor, he does what we want, and he has two years to prove himself. During the probation, if he preaches the way we want, sings the songs we like, lets us out when we want, and shows up and prays for us when we are in the hospital, then we may vote for him again. We just may keep him.

The truth is when the man of God is in the house, he is there because God sent him. He does not work for you. He works for God. When he speaks, it may not be what you want to hear but it is what God wants said. When he leads worship, he leads so Jesus can be glorified, not so everyone gets to sing his or her favorite.

The Old Testament prophet Isaiah promised the Kingdom of God would be governed by the Messiah, the Anointed One and Savior, God was sending. Ultimate fulfillment awaits Christ's Second Coming, but all power in Heaven and in earth belongs to Jesus even now.[23] His Kingdom exists wherever He is enthroned and nowhere should that be true more than in His Church.

Chapter 8
Real Power to the People!

Democracy run amok in the local church contradicts the popular notion of "power to the people." It actually throttles the flow of the only power that counts, God's power to meet needs.

Authority and spiritual power run on the same biblical track. Where the authority of Christ is flowing correctly, the power of His Resurrection can flow as well. The level of the miraculous is tied to the level of submission.

The principle of authority by submission is God ordained. In this context, surrendering to human authority requires faith in God. The believer must look beyond the personality and ideas of the pastor and trust the Giver of the office. Then, God can release to the individual the necessary authority for his or her own ministry responsibility.

That is what we mean by "theocracy." There is no pure theocracy today like Israel under God and Moses in the wilderness, but this is how God does church—dispensing His authority through His appointed and called representatives—this is theocracy.

Being a healthy, effective church demands this order because authority and divine power flow in tandem. People often wonder why more miracles seem to take place in nations other than the United States. At least one reason is that individuals in those lands, especially countries which are not democracies, understand submission to authority.

They know no other way. They submit to authority in the church and divine power flows. No one is distracted with "Well, I get my voice and vote. I get to make sure everyone knows what I think and how it affects me." Third World believers submit to authority from God, clearing the way for God's power to flow, and miracles unfold in that power.

To see the power of God evidenced in our churches, we must make a decision to let God re-establish the authority. He will call whomever He wills. We may question His choices, but it is not our call. He continues to confound the wise by using the foolish. God calls whom He wants and He gives authority to those whom He calls.

Matthew 8:8-10 beautifully illustrates this authority principle. The Roman officer asked Jesus for help but he refused the Lord's offer to go to his house. It was ceremonially unlawful for a Jew to enter a non-Jewish home, and the man knew he was unworthy of the Master's visit. He also knew it was not necessary.

> *The centurion replied, "Lord, I do not deserve to have you come under my roof. But just say the word, and my servant will be healed. For I myself am a man under authority, with soldiers under me. I tell this one, 'Go,' and he goes; and that one, 'Come,' and he comes. I say to my servant, 'Do this,' and he does it." When Jesus heard this, he was astonished and said to those*

following him, "I tell you the truth, I have not found anyone in Israel with such great faith.[24]

The centurion understood authority. His men obeyed him because his commands carried the weight of Caesar and the whole Roman Empire. He understood that Jesus, under God's authority, had all the power his servant needed, no matter the distance. "All you have to do is say the word and my servant will be healed," he declared.

Jesus stopped traffic at that statement! Matthew says He was "astonished." Jesus said, "I haven't found this kind of faith in all of Israel," and he used this to emphasize that believers from all nations would join the Jewish patriarchs at God's table.

This military man demonstrated faith that recognizes and submits to authority. You have to trust God to submit to the leadership He has sent to your church. If not, your issue is not only with the man of God but with the God of the man.

If you do not submit to God ordained authority in the house of the Lord, you will lose authority in your own house. When you stop submitting to the authorities God has placed in your life, those under your authority will not be able to submit to you. Your own children will abandon you because you did not treat the man of God the way He ordained, or they will follow your example and live in spiritual rebellion. That is the truth!

Since divine power and church authority flow on the same track, we have to get good at submission if we expect to experience God's power. Theocracy requires it.

Democracy is just the opposite. In the extreme, it says, "I get my way, my voice, and my vote, and I have my representative. I want to make sure they know what I am thinking. I didn't get to sit where I wanted and park where I wanted. This is my church and it's about me!" A church infected with that spirit is in the throes of death. If we are going to be healthy, we will have to do church God's way.

These principles grow even more exciting in light of Acts 2 and the outpouring of the Holy Spirit on the Day of Pentecost. God did not bring in just the Apostles and say, "I am going to use you in a mighty way and I want to fill you 12 with my Holy Spirit. Then, when you are about to die, you should bring in a dozen or so more and I will fill them ,so we will always have a few key people full of the Holy Spirit."

Everybody is welcome in the Upper Room. Christ told the 500 gathered when He ascended that they should stay in Jerusalem and wait for what His Father had promised. Interestingly, they did not all make it. Only 120 were still there when the Holy Spirit arrived, and all 120 were filled with the Spirit.

Were they the only ones who could receive? No! The previously embarrassed but now empowered Apostle Peter stepped forward to explain. "This is not just for this 120. This is for everyone! It's for Mommas and Daddies. It's for girls and for boys. It's for old people and for young people. It's for everybody from here on out, as many as the Lord our God shall call. Even though you weren't here and didn't get in on the ground floor, it is still available. Even now, if you will receive Christ, you can receive the power of the Holy Spirit."[25]

God fills believers with the Holy Spirit because every one of them is called to engage in ministry. Not just the 12 disciples, the 120, the pastor, or the evangelist, but the entire church should be in ministry. During the past 100 years, Pentecostals have become one of the fastest growing and largest segments of Christianity around the world. Why? Because the members, both by doctrine and by experience, take a personal responsibility for making Christ known.

As individual believers devote themselves to relevant service, they bring the power of God to bear on human need. Occasionally someone complains that they have had an experience with speaking in tongues but no power with it. Their problem may be that power is energy available to do work, not just a feeling.

Believers are not spiritual batteries to be charged for a buzz then held in reserve. We are conduits or circuits through which God's power can flow to meet needs. When the woman's desperate touch of faith brought her healing from 12 years of uncontrollable bleeding, Jesus realized "that power had gone out from him."[26]

Luke 6:19 records a tremendous moment in the earthly ministry of Jesus, "and the people all tried to touch him, because power was coming from him and healing them all." Successive waves of power flowed out of God's mercy to take away their sicknesses and pain!

Whether or not you feel power, God cannot use you to bring healing if you never go to the hurting. He cannot make you a soul-winner if you shun sinners, and you will not be energized for God's service until you reach out to people in need.

Dr. Earl Creps, author of *Off-Road Disciplines* and a student of postmodern culture, often counsels "seeker-sensitive" churches who feel a need to incorporate Baptism in the Holy Spirit and spiritual gifts into their ministry models. He poses the question, "First of all, are you doing anything dangerous enough that you need the Holy Spirit?"[27] If your church is not storming the gates of hell and your lifestyles and ministries do not provoke the devil, why should you worry about power?

Baptism in the Holy Spirit is God's power provision for each believer to get the job done. It is a powerful and healthy church where God's love flows through every member to meet human needs—where everyone is filled with the Spirit and in the ministry!

Chapter 9

What about Pastors Out of Control?

Now it is time to address the inevitable questions. "Doesn't absolute power corrupt absolutely? If we give our preacher too much power, he'll be ruined by it. Don't we owe it to him, to the church, and, yes, to God to oversee and hold him accountable?"

Uneasy church board members say things like, "We'll look up one day and he will have sold the van and gone on vacation.," or "He will hire somebody to do something with money we don't have…We're afraid! Absolute power corrupts. (It doesn't corrupt us, but…) It will mess him up."

You are right, it does corrupt. In fact, only one Person can handle absolute power and not be corrupted, Jesus Christ. That is why it belongs to Him alone. You are correct, too, that God structured the church so that no individual—preacher, deacon, or prominent member—has final authority.

No leader, at any level, can operate legitimately without practicing submission. Men and women called of God must submit to others called of God. They have authority only as they are under authority. There is no real power or authority for the maverick.

Every pastor needs advice and every good pastor knows it. Every gift God invests into each of His children carries a unique perspective, a specific way of looking at what the church faces. No one, not even the best pastor has universal perspective. No one can see from every angle. Wisdom demands a multitude of counselors.

God has placed incredible systems in His church so that unless I submit to the authority over me I stop having authority. Not just deacons to pastors, but pastors have to be in submission to those God has put over them.

The authors' fellowship, the General Council of the Assemblies of God, has a biblical credentialing process for individuals called to fulltime ministry. Other groups and congregations have similar systems or use some other method to accomplish the same purpose.

The Bible does not speak of ministerial credentials and the Early Church did not issue preaching licenses. It does, however, outline a process for launching God-called individuals into their ministries. The Scripture warns us not to lay hands on any man hastily.[28] This injunction does not mean, "Don't yield to the 'spirit of slap' if someone offends you," although that is good advice. It refers to ordaining individuals to serve the church.

Laying on of hands was but an external ceremony used in blessing and in ordination, or setting persons apart to some ecclesiastical employment... This the apostle forbids Timothy to do suddenly, that is, without a first proof of the person's fitness for his work, 1 Tim 3:10, both with respect to his knowledge, and to his holiness of conversation.[29]

One generation of called recognizes the next generation by the laying on of hands. They are not to do it in a hurry but are to give candidates time to mature in faith and service. Ordaining authorities are to make sure the call claimed is like their own. They are to make sure the individual has the quality of character and commitment required to carry this call. The life and labors of each one presenting himself for ordination must give evidence of the gifts and calling of God.

In our denomination, when a man or woman says, "God has called me to fulltime ministry," we set him or her down with a presbyter and committee to explore the possibility. One of the first questions will be, "How do you know you are called?"

The individual will tell his story of beginning to hear the voice of God. It may have come at summer camp, a special retreat, during a youth service, or with a pastor's sermon. It may have been ignited in times of personal prayer and Bible study, but he believes he can pursue no other path if he is to walk in the will of God.

With the endorsement of his pastor and his own convincing report, the committee will say, "We do believe God has His hand on you, and we want to help you explore and cultivate the calling." They will lay out requirements for Bible study and ministry training to make certain the individual develops effective preaching, teaching, and practical skills, "rightly dividing the Word of truth."[30]

During the proving process, letters of endorsement are collected from people inside and outside the local church. They must endorse the new minister's character, conduct and steadfast Christian commitment. They will report the growing evidence of God's call.

The process continues from level to level until the day of ordination. Then an elder, an ordained individual who has influenced the new minister's life, will lay hands upon him. The candidate kneels before the elder for a prayer of ordination.

The prayer of the elder with the laying on of hands confirms, "I see evidence of the same call that has been working in me these many years. Lord, I know, this young man, this young woman, has Your anointing. I recognize that call and anointing." The prayer is a commission and a charge, "In the name of Jesus Christ, the Head of the Church, I release you to fulfill the call of God. By that authority, GO!"

Young people start churches, go as missionaries, and do incredible things for God. That is how it is passed on. In the words of the Psalmist, "One generation shall commend your works to another, and shall declare your mighty acts."[31]

One day, Jesus Christ breathed on them and His disciples received His commission.[32] Later Peter, James, John, Paul, and that generation would lay their hands on the next generation. Then Timothy, Titus, and others would lay hands on the next generation, and so forth to the next and the next, until someone got to us. It has been passed on from generation to generation.

One young Methodist minister excited about his upcoming ordination said, "I'm only five hands from John Wesley!" He knew that the man who launched Methodism, John Wesley, had hands laid on him and he had laid hands on another and that one another through the generations. Now it was his turn!

His excitement almost makes me want to be a Methodist just to get in that line.

This is not to claim an "apostolic succession" for any individual or group of leaders. It is recognition of the unique privilege, responsibility, and accountability, as well as spiritual authority, of every individual called and commissioned to fulltime Christian service.

Ultimately, authority and power for ministry are conferred directly by Christ through the Holy Spirit. Of most importance is an immediate spiritual connection with Christ. "The living Lord of the Church is making direct, dynamic appointments in His body today."[33] Still, there is something wonderful about spiritual heritage and holding God's calling and blessings in common.

In a broader sense, every believer enjoys this spiritual heritage in the celebration, memorial, and testimony of Holy Communion. Taking the cup and the bread, we identify with every generation of believers since those who took them from the hand of Jesus Christ Himself. We recognize our link with every follower of Christ around the world. We declare our unity, equality, and interdependence as we look for our Lord's return.

However, the laying on of hands is not just recognition of the call and official release to the fullness of ministry. It is taking responsibility for them. The ordaining elders become responsible. Admonishing Timothy, and through his letter, all other church authorities not to commission anyone ill-equipped, unqualified, or unprepared for ministry, Paul added the reason. "Neither be partaker of other men's sins."

This has been readily understood through the centuries. Puritan preacher and theologian Matthew Poole wrote in the mid-1600s:

> *He who puts into the ministry any erroneous or ignorant persons, or any persons of a lewd conversation, makes himself guilty of all the harm they do, if he hath not first taken a due and reasonable proof of them, but hath laid hands upon them suddenly. Amongst other ways by which we interest ourselves in others' guilt, one is, by not hindering it, having power so to do. He, or they, whom it lies upon to admit, or not admit, men into the ministry, have a power to refuse them in case upon proof of them they do not find them apt to teach, or fit for the ministration they are to undertake, or such for holiness of life as God requireth...[34]*

In the Old Testament, the priesthood was responsible for the priesthood. The people did not exercise oversight of the priests. In the New Testament Church, the called of God, oversaw the called of God. That is how it is today. If a pastor gets out of line, if he does something he should not, the remedy is not petition and ballot but apostolic authority in the denomination, fellowship, or pastors of other churches covenanted for oversight.

In the Assemblies of God, individuals concerned about a minister's conduct would contact the sectional presbyter. The denomination in the United States is divided into districts comprised of geographic regions or combinations of language and geographic areas. Each district is led by a district superintendent and he is assisted by presbyters who oversee the district sections. All a concerned individual in the local church should have to do is contact the sectional presbyter.

He or she should express the causes for concern, "Our pastor is doing some stuff that we've never seen before and he is saying some stuff that we can't find in the Bible. We are a little concerned that our pastor may be off the mark. Would you come check it out?"

The first thing the presbyter, as an agent of the district, would do, of course, is check out the source of the complaint. He would need to confirm that it is a credible report. No one should send an anonymous letter or call if he is not willing to identify himself. If a situation warrants attention, the trustworthy individual will bow up and do what is needed for the sake of God's work. He will be willing, so to speak, to put his own neck on the line.

When the presbyter receives such a call with proper identification and contact information, he will look into the situation. If the caller proves credible and other witnesses concur with his concern, the presbyter will check out the pastor to see whether the report is correct.

If it is accurate, one of two things will happen. Depending upon the nature and degree of the problem, the district may help the pastor to make corrections while he continues to lead the church. If what he is doing is putting the sheep in danger, the district will act in behalf of the flock and remove him.

After that, the district would continue to work with the pastor for personal and ministerial restoration. Should he be unwilling to repent and submit to a restorative process, the district would do as the Bible says, treat him like a "pagan and a tax collector,"[35] and dismiss him from affiliation. That would be his call.

Other denominations have similar processes for accountability and effective non-denominational or unaffiliated congregations put processes in place for ministerial accountability.

What are legitimate causes for concern about a pastor? Overseeing authorities need to know about unscriptural preaching and teaching, immoral or unethical conduct, or ministerial incompetence. If any of these occur, it is time to call the appropriate outside authority. That is the way that is right.

The Old Testament Book of 1 Samuel, chapters 24 and 26, gives good examples of these principles. King Saul had disobeyed God and fallen from divine favor. David had been anointed to become king but Saul still occupied the throne.

Saul still had the position of authority but he had forfeited the divine sanction. His rebellion led to bitterness and anger that affected everyone and everything around him.

The worst preacher in the world is one who still is the pastor but who no longer has God's anointing. He becomes mean and nobody wants to work for him. He treats his staff badly, he mistreats his church, and he neglects or abuses his family. When a pastor loses the anointing, he becomes a problem for everybody. Pastor, if you have lost the anointing, go into the prayer closet and don't come out until you get it!

God delivered Saul into David's hands, twice. David could have taken it upon himself to solve the nation's leadership problem. He had the anointing. He could have claimed the position. His men urged, "Kill him!" and "Let me kill him!" But David refused! He even repented for surreptitiously cutting off the corner of the king's robe.

Even though Saul no longer served under God's favor, David knew it was not his place to remove the king. He honored Saul because once he had been anointed to lead. If David had violated the authority over him, he would have had no authority of his own.

Likewise, it is not the job of the church to fix the pastor. The authority flows from above. It is the job of those with an apostolic oversight to deal with him. Call them and let them do it.

Unfortunately, here is what often happens. Disgruntled or hurting people think, "Our bylaws say we can get a petition, have a meeting, and call in our pastor..." Yes, you can, but if you do, you will damage the church to the point it will take years to restore it to what God established it to do.

When you reach up to take down the shepherd, the whole church suffers. It is much better to look to those who have that authority and responsibility. Let them deal with it, and the church can move on to find God's choice to take the place of the one who failed. Or, maybe, the pastor can be restored and returned to effective service.

Please hear the heart of this district leader. It echoes the cry of church leaders and wounded congregations across the nation. We are ready to have healthy churches. We are weary of churches needing healing because of a pastor or board or how they dealt with a pastor or board. There is a right way to do everything.

We long for the churches to be healthy and we want power in your altars and power in your pews. We want everyone in your church to be in the ministry and the authority to be where it belongs.

Pastor, you have the authority in the church, but please understand you don't have all the answers. The Bible teaches clearly there is wisdom in the multitude of counselors. Deacons, submit to that authority, but help your pastor see with wisdom and work together to be all God wants His church to be.

Chapter 10

How Churches Become Deacon-Possessed

Churches usually do not create entrenched boards, and problem deacons may not start that way. They evolve. A variety of negative processes moves them from spiritual ministry to carnal maneuvering.

Initially, when a church elects a group of deacons to serve as an official board and leadership team to work with the pastor, it is close to biblical purity. They have a good pastor. They have good leadership, and they are a spiritually healthy congregation. At times, it is like the Book of Acts with pastor and deacons in place, ministry authority properly flowing, and the church growing. Then a series of events unfolds to change the picture.

At least four situations may tempt deacon boards to overstep their biblical bounds. One or more occur at some time in the life of almost every church. They include resignation of the pastor, moral failure by a pastor, relocation of a board member or leader, or a lapse in pastoral leadership by a misinformed man of God.

When a Pastor Resigns

A common event which sets some churches on the wrong course of authority is resignation of the pastor. He may leave to serve another congregation, take another ministry post, or retire. Whatever the reason, he leaves the position of authority as pastor, and the deacons find themselves responsible for overseeing the church and all its ministries.

This creates a sensitive and vulnerable time for the church. Often the board faithfully carries out its responsibilities, leads a fruitful search for God's choice, and surrenders authority to the new shepherd. If not, trouble begins.

Sometimes board members enjoy their situation, and they should. They thrill to hear the voice of God and share it with the people. The Lord speaks to them and gives them direction because He loves His church, but that does not mean they are to keep the position or have the authority in the house. It does not belong to them.

If the deacons lose sight of this fact and relish the power, if they enjoy feeling important with the people coming to them, they risk taking the first step to disrupting the church life and health. They may drag their feet in the pastoral search and, when finally they do find the right pastor, they may not give back all the authority. They may keep some for themselves.

Somewhere in the transition they have decided they are pretty good at this. They feel they have the right answers. They move themselves up in their own minds and in church authority. So, the second pastor does not receive the full authority of the first.

This process can continue three or four elections deep to diminish the pastor's role to hireling shepherd. It produces a revolving door of short term pastors because each transition reinforces the illicit power base. The church no longer looks for a pastor to lead them. They want someone only to preach and do what they want done.

Churches in this all too common trap rob their communities of fruitful ministries and shut their doors to needy people. The gates of hell will not prevail against Christ's Church, but this subtle power encroachment brings a local church down from the inside.

When a Pastor Fails

A second situation which results in a shift of authority from the biblical channels is moral failure on the part of the pastor. When the local church shepherd falls into sin, the trust factor plummets for all preachers.

The next pastor doesn't have a chance. Even though he brings a great track record, has proven trustworthy and faithful in godly living and leadership elsewhere, he is suspect in the wounded church.

Much like the woman who distrusts all men or the man who denounces all women because the one they loved betrayed them, board members and congregations seek to shield themselves from further pain. It defies logic, but they group all pastors with the one who has failed.

When that happens, the board members may find it in their hearts to redefine their roles. They suddenly feel it is their responsibility to keep the church pastor in line, to make certain he does not do anything amiss. Without trust, he cannot lead, they will not follow, and the church will flounder through a succession of ineffective and frustrated pastors.

When Board Members Move

A third scenario that disrupts the proper flow of authority can occur when board members change churches. A deacon, or another person in leadership, who has been affected by a pastoral failure or infected by an authoritative board, may be elected to office in a new church. He or she can bring the unhealthy perspective to the new congregation. It may have nothing to do with that local church but something has happened to the individual which he transfers to his new position.

The relocated deacon will begin trying to give direction, not just advice, to his new pastor. He moves out of the position God called him to fill and adopts an overseer mentality. To him, it is justified by his previous experience. He believes God wants him or the church needs him to do this. In fact, many malfunctioning deacons are good people just thinking wrong. Either way, he becomes a problem rather than a help for the pastor and people.

When a Pastor Misunderstands

Churches also may get upside down in authority when pastors misunderstand or abnegate their role as overseer. Sometimes well-meaning pastors train board members to be representatives of the people. They cultivate the mindset "you will be here though pastors come and go."

This may seem to work well under that pastor. He has cultivated good relationships and developed trust with positive experience, but he is planting dangerous seeds for succeeding pastors.

If board members rise to the role for which they erroneously have been groomed, they may refuse to submit to a new pastor's vision. Ultimately the church is split or stifled, and a misguided man of God started the process.

Supporting the pastor is the primary work of the deacon. If he instead exerts his own authority, for whatever reason, the church will suffer. Good deacons wrap their hands and their hearts around the fact that they help the pastor push back the enemy, and the whole church walks in blessing.

Chapter 11

When Churches Are Deacon-Blessed

A pastor and board functioning correctly make a powerful team. The deacons hold up their shepherd's hands the way Aaron and Hur supported Moses when God's people battled the Amalekites.[36] So long as Moses extended the rod of God, the symbol of his divine call and authority, the Israelites won. When his hands dropped, the enemy prevailed, so the leaders by his side kept Moses' hands held high.

When the pastor is lifted up, the whole church goes to a new level. When the pastor is pushed down, the church goes with him. Deacons have a multifaceted role, but the heart of it is to support and assist the pastor. They do that in prayer. They also do it as in Acts 6 where the seven men chosen to serve went to work in the daily food distribution. Some of the deacons began laying hands on the sick and God multiplied the ministry of the church with miracles and other manifestations of the Spirit.

Deacons have a legal function we cannot overlook. In the United States, the church is a tax-exempt non-profit organization under Section 501(c) (3) of the Internal Revenue Code. It must be managed in compliance with IRS regulations. You will not find anyone better to meet those requirements than good deacons.

They are spiritually mature and trustworthy individuals with a deep personal commitment to the church's mission. They are integrally involved in its life and ministries. Good deacons will meet and exceed all the government expects of an organizational board.[37]

It is a problem, of course, if these individuals become more board than deacon oriented. They disqualify themselves because what makes them worthy to serve on the organizational board is the biblical standard for deacons.

As those qualities unfold, blessings flow to the church, the community, and beyond. When the man God has sent to a city as pastor is undergirded and walking in the right authority, he literally can push back the darkness and bring light to the community. Faithful deacons push with him.

Much like a local church should function, Moses gave the people God's plan then watched over the battle in the power and authority God had given him. The people did the work! Under the covering of the divine commission, they advanced, but when Moses let down the rod, they began to lose ground. Those closest to him kept his hands lifted. This is the job of the deacon today.

Deacons bless the church as they reinforce the pastor in four essential ways: They pray for him, they extend his ministry arms, and they add their unique perspectives to perfect his vision. Then deacons bless the church and back their pastor most tangibly when they set his salary.

When Deacons Pray

First of all, they pray! No one should pray for the pastor more than the deacons. They grasp the power of prayer and how God responds, then take the lead in intercession. They each spend time daily praying for the pastor and come together for regular prayer times to support him.

When Deacons Are the Pastor's Hands

Second, deacons extend the pastor's hands in service. They go out and touch people, meet needs, mow lawns—whatever is needed. They do it in the name of the Lord but also in the name of the pastor. Deacons are the fingers and feet of his vision!

When the pastor raises his hands to God's purpose, good deacons multiply them. A large part of the deacon's ministry extends beyond the immediate task to organizing others and helping lead them in service. When the pastor holds forth, the entire body of Christ goes to work. When he reaches out, everything moves forward. The deacons make that happen.

Deacons take what the pastor is being led to do and spread it through the body. They add specific administrative, motivational, and organizational skills to make sure it comes to pass. They do not oppose what he is doing—unless as prescribed in previous chapters.

When Deacons Are the Pastor's Eyes

Third, the deacon blesses the church as he becomes the pastor's eyes. This means each deacon sees from his experience, gifting, and perspective what others may not realize. He can say: "Pastor, in all honesty, I'm seeing this, hearing this, and from my perspective, I suggest…"

Every gift of God for service brings a unique way of looking at everything. Responsibility for the work and his strong leadership gifts moved the Apostle Paul to refuse a vacillating John Mark a place on his missionary team.[38] Barnabus, with his gifts for consolation, saw a promising young worker in need of a mentor. The results were a stronger missionary force, led by Paul and Silas, for the immediate project but also a restored young preacher whom Paul later found of great value.[39]

The pastor has only his perspective. Good deacons can see things which may escape him in the same event or circumstances. Deacons also are circulating in places and engaging in activities beyond the pastor's circuit. This is why there is wisdom in the multitude of counselors.

Knowing this, deacons sit at planning tables with specific insights. They should share candidly, "Pastor, I see it this way" and "It appears to me…" This is not to override the pastor but to give him the full information he needs as he works to hear the voice of God.

Wisdom comes in three ways: experience, counsel, and the Lord's direction. First is experience. A man learns from what he has done, heard, seen, or read. It develops in him a certain level of human wisdom. Everyone has some of this. Next is wisdom of the group. It comes through the insight and advice of many counselors. The third and greatest source of wisdom is the Lord Himself.

The goal of the pastor, and those working with him, is to come to the wisdom of God. As deacons work together with him, really love him, and faithfully stand with him to hold up his hands, they offer the completed perspective he desperately needs.

So, deacons are the pastor's hands and eyes, serving as a buffer between the mundane stuff of church life and the real stuff the pastor needs to do. They help make sure he does not bog down in anything that would keep him from being fully able to love, lead, teach, and do the main things God has sent him to do. He must always be free to preach and teach the Word and to lead the church.

When Deacons Set the Pastor's Salary

A fourth way deacons bless the church is in setting the pastor's salary. Deacons typically have the duty and sacred responsibility of deciding how and what the pastor will be paid. They bless or bind the church immeasurably by how they do it.

Paul makes clear to Timothy that the pastor who does his work well, especially preaching and teaching, is worthy of double honor.[40] He should receive "twice as much" or "a much greater" reward for his service.

The Greek word here for "honor" means "value" or "price". The context relates it to the pastor's salary or support.[41] Paul's teaching may seem self-serving, but a higher principle is at stake.

How much is the pastor worth to you? What value do you place on God's gift to the church? If the church is operating correctly, your children will live better lives. Your grandchildren will live better lives. They will go to heaven, and you will go to heaven when you die. Your community is going to become more righteous because of a good pastor. You will live in a better neighborhood. There will be peace in the house of God and it will filter into your home. The man of God will share incredible wisdom, priceless Bible teaching, and a shepherd's love for his flock. Miracles are going to come when you appreciate the gift God has given.

When you love, respect, and value the gift from God, you will not want to know how cheaply you can get by in paying a pastor. The mindset to pay the least a pastor will accept or to "go for the cheap one" among candidates demonstrates you do not value the call of God and His pastor-teacher gift.

True deacons lift the hands of the pastor. They bring the perspective for strong support and they will not be stingy. They will take the Scriptures to heart and determine to bless the pastor as they would bless the Lord. They will prove their appreciation for His gift.

If a board and the church are not generous with His gift, why would He be generous with them? If the person God has sent is not rightly honored, how can he lead and direct the body as he should? The whole understanding that God gives a pastor to lead, bless, and take the church into a new place in His purpose begins here.

What about the other side of the issue? Suppose the church blesses and shows great respect for the gift, but that pastor does not prove worthy. Wise deacons know God sees the heart. If the church honors the office and God's call, He will give them a pastor who will live up to and exceed all they are willing to pay. If you do right because it is right, God will make sure you have a worthy individual who will a blessing to you and to your community. Do not wait until you get the right person. Start now being generous.

Some individuals and churches practice the dangerous notion of withholding tithes so the pastor cannot make it. They intend to starve him out. They are playing desperate games with God. Ananias and Sapphira paid a terrible price for holding back and lying to the Holy Spirit.[42] Their sin may not have been a church power grab, but the same selfish and rebellious spirit was at work. If a man needs to go, address the problem the right way. Look to those overseeing him in authority for help, but always honor the office.

In matters of salary, deacons deal with holy things, the Lord's tithe and how He would spend it. Good deacons make certain they keep right purpose and pure motives as they take action on salary for the person God has called to lead them. Then they bless, not just the pastor, but the whole church.

Chapter 12

A Healthy Board Meeting

What does a healthy board meeting look like? More than a parliamentary model, it must be a reflection of a healthy pastor-board relationship. This means intercession, powerful and regular times of praying together. It is fellowship inside and outside the board room with recreation, fun times, and sometimes just hanging out together. It will mean times of casting vision then Spirit-guided development and implementation of a plan.

The bond between the pastor and board members calls for mutual respect, candor, and confidence. Cultivating all these elements will result in healthy and productive sessions. You will give necessary oversight to the church operations and budgets, but you will not bog down in money or other issues.

A healthy board meeting gives first priority to fervent prayer. The main job is to connect with God. It is His work and the flow of His Holy Spirit is the only way it can be done. Everything the pastor and board do is about Him and what He wants.

Second, the meeting should foster fellowship. Allow time to care for one another. The pastor and all the deacons should enjoy being and working together.

Third, the pastor should unfold his vision for the church. In an atmosphere of intercession and fellowship, he readily can share what the Lord is telling him, and the deacons can add their insights. Of course, God will tell the pastor very little if he is not spending his own time in prayer.

In Sachse, the board would help shape and implement vision. I would spell out where I felt God leading us. Then we would work on it together. The deacons did not oppose or try to change it, but they would respond from their own perspectives. Different ones would ask, "Have you thought about …?" and would give new insights. The various points of view inherent in their gifts would help flesh out and finalize the vision. Again and again, they proved there really is wisdom in the multitude of counselors!

Next, we would talk about how to do it. The board members would ask how to get there, and we would work on the best way to move forward in what God was leading us to do. They would begin to take responsibility for parts of the vision according to their gifts, abilities, schedules, and skills. They would volunteer, "I'm going to do this, this, and this."

The specific discussion would become a distribution of authority and they would each become responsible for various parts of the vision. The authority was with me as pastor, I delegated it to them, and they would carry it out.

Once a quarter we went over the finances. Every board member received a summary each month of income, expenses and balances, but we went over the quarterly reports to make sure we stayed in line with our budget. As pastor and board, we approved the budget each year. Once it was adopted, it was just a matter of making sure we stayed true to it. We did not have to talk about money all the time.

A key element to casting and pursuing vision is having the right individuals on the church staff. When I was hiring, I would ask the deacons to do an interview. I had the authority as pastor, but I was wise enough to realize these men may see things I miss. Also, I wanted them on board with me. For the same reasons, I kept them informed when it was necessary to terminate staff.

We would do these things together though everyone understood the decisions were mine. The process worked and it was healthy because of the relationship we enjoyed. The deacons and other leaders knew they had great influence in my life. Their perspectives mattered to me.

If major issues arise for any church, usually that means somebody does something stupid. Deacons can help deal with those things. Church boards have to take care of church business, but that is not why you meet. It is just one of the things you do.

A good relationship—spending time together playing golf, eating dinner, visiting each other's homes, plus incredible times of prayer—will culminate in healthy and fruitful board meetings. The purpose is mission, vision, direction, and the health of the church.

Chapter 13

When Should the People Vote?

When and upon what should people of the church vote? This is a good question but one without specific Bible directives. The New Testament does not give election instructions or advance a specific model for making decisions in the congregation. This allows the church to thrive in any culture and any age. Whatever the process may be for the whole church to make decisions, the goal and guiding principle is to arrive at God's choice.

In Acts 1, the body of believers addressed the vacancy among the 12 Apostles created by the fall of Judas. They recognized from the Scriptures the necessity for action and they established the qualifications before they chose candidates. To be counted among The Twelve who would give eye-witness testimony of Jesus Christ, the new Apostle would have to be one who had walked with Him from John's baptism to the Resurrection.[43]

The believers prayed for God to make known His choice as they cast lots:

> *"Lord, you know everyone's heart. Show us which of these two you have chosen to take over this apostolic ministry, which Judas left to go where he belongs."*

Then they cast lots, and the lot fell to Matthias; so he was added to the eleven apostles. Acts 1:24-26

This is the last instance in the Bible of casting lots to make decisions.

In Acts 6, believers again were called upon to make choices impacting the whole church. The Apostles told them to choose seven men to be appointed to oversee the daily food distribution.[44] By whatever means they arrived at their choices, and before they acted, the Apostles laid out the requirements. The men picked were to be full of the Holy Spirit, full of wisdom, and fully recognized for those qualities.[45]

Everything which may call for a vote from the congregation, first of all, requires a set of standards and prerequisites for the process. These will enable us to move forward in whatever way is best to reach a conclusion.

New Testament churches are to rely upon God's Word, to seek God's will in prayer, and to expect to confirm it in the expression of the body. The Word and what I truly believe God wants in the immediate situation, after honest and fervent prayer, must inform my vote. When believers ballot, it is not for personal preference but to bear out what we trust to be God's will for His church.

With this understanding, we can consider recommendations as to when and for what the people should vote. Three instances stand out. First, any time a lot of money is to be expended, a vote is in order. Second, when it is time to name a new pastor, a voice from the body is good, and third, selection of deacons calls for input from the congregation.

Simple wisdom and sound leadership dictate a vote when we ask the church to spend large sums. As pastor, I need to know I have shared the vision correctly and completely. I need to know the members are on board. If they vote "no," it is because I have not effectively communicated what God has put into my heart.

"Large" expenditures would include real estate purchases, construction of new buildings, any long term financial obligations, or anything, more or less, of permanence for the church. If the people must live with it or pay for it for a long time, they should vote.

This does not include vehicles, equipment, or ministry supplies. Depending upon the size of the church and the budget, a van might be a big thing. The guideline for a call to vote hinges on what will commit a major portion of the church income. Again, it does not include necessities for on-going ministry.

In each case, as the pastor, I need to have the backing of the body because I do not want to divide the church. Good leadership produces strong "follower-ship." If I have done a good job, by the time we vote, we all will be acting together.

This kind of vote lets members know I value their opinion. It does not diminish the authority of the pastor or imply the church is a democracy where everything is by majority rule. If I cross that line, I mess up everything

In the matter of choosing a new pastor, the church is well-served when the congregation is involved. The Scriptures do not prescribe a process. They establish qualifications for candidates. Pastors named in the New Testament appear to have been appointed and commissioned by the Apostles and/or presbyters. Some denominations today follow a similar system to appoint or install local pastors.

We believe it is better to let the church find the one who best fits. They can arrive at what they believe to be God's choice with the help and then the blessing of the outside leadership. If the people are denied a ballot in what is perhaps the most important decision for a church, they may vote with their feet. The congregation needs to be involved and, ultimately, there should be an up or down vote on one qualified candidate.

The pulpit committee and the church make a dangerous mistake to pit two or more candidates against each other as a democratic contest. One group in the church will connect with one candidate and other groups will back another.

When the election is over, no matter who wins, someone has lost. The new pastor is being called to lead a divided congregation, including one or more groups who did not want him. This is common in national politics, one party in and the losers out, but it is devastating in the church. Though Christ may enact His will within any system, it is hard to imagine any process pleases Him which cultivates division in His church.

Those in leadership prayerfully and carefully should select one person whom they feel God would send to their church. They should recommend that candidate to the body. Then the church should pray and consider whether they agree.

Once they vote, the church moves on under the new pastor. If the vote is "No," that candidate may not return for consideration, and the search committee repeats the process. As a church, we walk away and start again.

This way we keep the body in unity. There is no value in creating a democratic contest. A voice is good, but the purpose always is to confirm what we believe God wants. Then the authority properly is placed with the new shepherd.

The church body also should be involved in selecting deacons, at least, in the nominating process. The same tendencies for division may prevail in full election of deacons as do with multiple candidates for pastors. The unelected and their supporters feel rejected.

A variety of approaches seem to work well with some basic principles in common. The church cast lots in Acts 1 to put the choice of the new Apostle in God's hands, but they carefully qualified the individuals whose names they put into the hat. Likewise with the seven servants or deacons in Acts 6, they established the prerequisites before choosing.

Some churches take nominations for deacon from the congregation. Then the board interviews nominees to establish both their qualifications and their willingness to serve. The vetted names are brought to the body in a business meeting for an election.

In other churches, the people nominate, the board qualifies, and the church approves a list of candidates. Then those already serving select from the list the ones to replace those leaving the board.

Many churches present the list of qualified nominees and allow their pastor to select the new board members. This is both scriptural and practical. The pastor is the one who will have to work most closely with them. A negative factor, of course, is that he cannot pick everyone. Those not chosen may feel rejected. It is hard to eliminate every sense of competition, but mature believers will keep in focus what is best for the church.

Chapter 14
Becoming a Church that Works

Becoming a church that works begins with the pastor. He must live the model before he can lead and expect people to follow. He must submit to the authority God has designed for him and earn trust with love and faithful service. He needs to teach at every level so the people drive change with their own grasp of the biblical process. For the church to work, the pastor and the people have to focus on the lost.

Living the model starts with the pastor putting himself clearly under the authority of an apostolic body. This means someone sent from God to hold him accountable for his life and ministry. Theocracy never is without cover. Abraham, father of nations[46] and the friend[47] of God, paid tithes to Melchizedek. He submitted to a person as a representative of God. [48]

Absolute power does corrupt, and aligning with God's flow of authority does not give anyone the right to do as he or she pleases. This book is not about empowering pastors. It is about bringing Christ's will to His Church and His work to the world.

Pastor, if you do not have an apostolic covering, ask God to show you whom He has chosen for that function. Often, it is an obvious lineage or spiritual family tree within the group in which you came to know Christ. Sometimes it is not. God led

Abraham away from his family because He was doing something new in him. God will help you as you seek to follow His process. When you know the proper authority, you must submit as unto the Lord.

When the church sees their pastor in submission to authority, they have an example to follow. If they see a self-serving doing-his-own-thing leader, they will follow that example. The pastor must practice what he wants to reproduce.

The next prerequisite for building the church that works is trust. People believe those whom they respect and trust. Whatever they believe, true or not, they hold because they learned it from someone they trusted, or because a leader they trusted took advantage of them. Either way, the pastor will not be able to lead people into truth until he proves trustworthy.

How can he do that? He should live up to their legitimate expectations. The people rightly expect their pastor to be a man of prayer. He should be faithful to daily times of meeting with God, talking to God, and hearing from God in the secret place. Public change and lasting results in his ministry result from private prayer.

Similarly, the people expect their pastor to study, prepare, and faithfully preach and teach the Bible, the whole will of God.[49] To merit their trust, he will be diligent in preparation and in every presentation of the Word.[50] The fire of God will burn in his spirit. The Word of God will be in his mouth, and the love of God will flow from his heart.

The people also expect their shepherd to be available to them in times of need, to keep office hours, and to care when they are hurting. The trustworthy pastor will surpass their hopes.

Being a pastor in a small community may call for less time in the office but not less time at work. The rural pastor serves the whole community and each day includes a circuit of ministry and cultivating relationships. After daily prayer and study times, he goes to where the people are, downtown or in the fields, to connect both with church folks and the unchurched to help meet needs.

The people of any church expect their pastor to be an integral part of their lives in good times and bad. He performs weddings, dedicates their children and grandchildren, baptizes family members, and celebrates with them the happy events in their lives. He also goes to them when they are hurting. This means hospital visits, waiting room vigils, funerals, and times of praying and weeping together for God's comfort and peace.

If the people find their pastor dependable when and where they think he should be, then they will transfer that trust to other areas. They will be convinced he cares about them.

Trust comes as people know their pastor loves them and wants only what is good. If they test that love and he fails, he will not be able to lead. Building trust takes time, and there is no shortcut to a long time.

Whatever it takes, the people must be convinced of the pastor's love. He cannot come in and announce changes just because he knows they need to be made. The primary concern of many members is that he has an ulterior motive for tampering with what they have been doing for years. He has to form a trusting relationship by taking time to love them.

He builds credibility by pouring his life into them and pouring himself out for them. Alton Garrison, assistant general superintendent of the Assemblies of God, tells pastors that people will not do new or different things "until you have invested more in them than it will cost them to change."[51]

The congregation may love and respect their pastor from day one, and they should. He can enjoy a productive pastorate from the very beginning. Still, it takes years to experience enough of life together for the preacher to become "Pastor" in their hearts. Members will not open to him the deepest areas of their lives until he proves worthy of their confidence.

After more than three years with a wonderful congregation, I was both taken aback and blessed by the comment of a charter member. The church had treated us royally, good things had happened, and she always had been one of our strongest supporters. So I was surprised when she told me I finally had become their pastor. She said, "You've always been good, but now I can see your pastor's heart unfolding."

When the pastor knows that the people know he loves them, he can begin to announce change. In the context of love and trust, they are more likely to respond with, "We know he cares about us. That makes what he's doing worth following."

A common mistake young or new pastors make is to start changing things the day they arrive. They assume they can because they hold the pastor's position. They learn all too quickly, sometimes painfully, that they are in no position to lead transition until they have trust. The people may not be hostile to them personally so much as wary of unwarranted change. The wise pastor will take time to lead in love. He will deal with what is there until he builds the credibility to change it.

As the pastor models submission and earns trust with love and service, he also must fill the process for change with teaching. The people must understand the reasons for change, that God has set in place a flow of authority and that He has called each of them to minister.

As pastor in Sachse, I taught a lot on ministry gifts from the Father. I tried my best to empower people and keep them focused on ministry for their sakes and for the Kingdom. We developed a lot of ministries, a lot of outreaches, because the people were much more concerned about winning souls than who was in charge at the church. This also allowed us to focus on missions. The church became a leader in our denomination in giving to world ministries because we weren't wrapped up in ourselves.

If the pastor teaches correctly in every proper setting and at all levels, the people eventually will embrace it and become advocates for change. He teaches, teaches, and teaches some more—on Sunday mornings, in small groups, in leadership meetings, and one-to-one in fellowship—until the people begin to call for change. Not everyone will get on board, but enough will take hold of the concepts that change can begin in response to their calls and not out of the blue.

When they say, "Pastor, we believe it should be this way," they are parroting the truths he is pouring into them. Then he can agree. When they say, "That's not how we do it," he can ask, "Why don't we fix it?" Because he teaches consistently and lovingly over a long enough period, these believers actually will bring about the necessary change.

This is successful change. If the pastor attempts it without teaching, then the people will not grasp the reasons and will find it very hard to do anything different. Knowing the need and being motivated by it is more important for the people than the mechanism or procedure by which change takes place.

Becoming a church that works does not start with the constitution and bylaws. It is changing attitudes, opinions, and understanding. When that happens, the documents will fall into place. If the pastor attempts to change the bylaws too fast, the church may change pastors even faster. In other words, do not ask people to vote on giving up their vote

A final but overriding principle for becoming the church that works is that the pastor and the people must focus on the lost. The church exists to deliver the message of Jesus Christ to everyone everywhere.

This is one of the greatest lessons we learned at Sachse Assembly. When you make and maintain the focus on lost people, never the people who already are there, it keeps the church healthy. The people did not try to run the church but devoted themselves to being servants and witnesses. As a result, the church multiplied. The people stayed in ministry and leadership stayed leadership. (For more about this point and others, read Appendix 1, *Lessons from the Sachse Experience)*

We did not have money so everyone had to have a job, and church was all about ministry. Each person got involved in mowing, cleaning, keeping kids, keeping the books, leading worship, or something. We had more job opportunities, more things that needed to be done, than we had people. So, everyone took part in ministry.

This book is designed to help pastors, leaders, and individual believers take hold of the principles and experience the power of doing church God's way. The video supported training course and study guide offer practical tools for becoming *The Church that Works!* Getting it right really does release the people of God into ministry, and it unleashes the power of God to work with them.

Appendix 1

Lessons from the Sachse Experience

In 1987, Sachse Assembly of God was a struggling congregation of fewer than 20 members in a city of about 5,000 people on the northeastern edge of Dallas, Texas. Church attendance grew over the next 17 years to more than 800 each week as the congregation and church leaders embraced and applied biblical principles for a healthy church. Explosive growth continues with weekly attendance in 2009 of more than 1800. The following lessons from the Sachse experience are drawn from a question and answer session on Democracy vs. Theocracy before work began on *The Church that Works!*

Mel: What factors were in place at Sacshe Assembly that helped make it possible to implement biblical principles and practices?

Rick: It was brand new, not a new church, but with only 17 people, it wasn't a huge crowd, and they were desperate. There was a new desperation which quickly changed to a new church vision and commitment. We, all of us, wanted to build a new church impacting the whole area for God. So I didn't have to fight the established system.

Then, the church grew by new people and the new people came in under Bible teaching for a church that works. They learned how the church should function and we were able to grow it from the ground. I learned also as we moved forward.

If I had been in a church where I had to fight for change while I was still learning, I don't know that we would have gotten there so well. Now, I believe I am in a position to help other churches. The number one factor in our favor was not having an old control base. Where that does exist, those involved need to search their hearts and come to the place where what Christ wants for His church is all that matters.

Church leaders and members need to ask themselves, "If there were no church here, what would we do to reach this city for Jesus?" They should answer that question by considering others, "If we were the church God wants us to be, what would we look like and what would we be doing?" Honest answers followed by positive actions will result in a healthy new church.

In Sachse, the people we reached were very young and they weren't set in their ways. We were able to look for truth together without having to defend something handed down to us. In terms of democracy vs. theocracy and not voting on every matter, I've had some later to argue that the biblical way is to vote. They really believe there is a Scripture that teaches everybody is supposed to get a vote and, if not, they want to vote anyway! So, I have dealt with those issues, but we didn't have any of that in place at the outset. That really allowed us to do what was needed.

Mel: What factors tended to hinder the process of becoming a church that works?

Rick: The only times we had battles were when people came from other churches, who did not get saved at Sachse, if they brought with them a different mindset of how church is supposed to be. Some strong independent churches had been very much congregational along with the majority of Baptists and Assemblies of God churches. If they brought that perspective, as we would move forward, some would question why we operated the way we did. They would want us to change. We had some confrontation, but it never gained a foothold because we started, or restarted, correctly.

It was interesting that people really would be offended by the fact they didn't get to vote on every $100 spent or have a voice in staffing and every ministry matter. I realized they were not coming to win souls. They were coming to vote. They were coming to be leaders, not followers, because that's how they were raised. We would combat that by saying, "This is how we do it here, but there are many churches that do it that way. If that's what you're looking for, we can give you a list of places you might be more comfortable." We were determined to stick with what we believed God had put into our hearts. God blessed at Sachse and He's still blessing in an incredible way.

Mel: What were the results?

Rick: First of all, we were able to do what God was leading us to do without a lot of fanfare. We just could do it. We were allowed to make mistakes, and everybody would say, "Oh well, let's try another one." It really created an atmosphere conducive to trying things we'd never done. If it didn't work, we didn't have to go back to the body for another plan. We did a lot of new things and a lot of the things we did worked really well. The atmosphere was there for success.

We ended up with a lot of people involved in ministry because they understood that their purpose was ministry, not just leadership but every kind of ministry—in worship, small groups, children's ministry, the church office and a whole spectrum of activities to touch people with God's love. I taught a lot on gifts from the Father and I tried my best to empower people and keep them focused on ministry for their sake and the sake of the kingdom.

Because our people concerned themselves with winning others to Jesus, we were able to focus on reaching the lost around the world. We became very strong in missions giving and even going because we weren't wrapped up in ourselves. I think all of that, the level of getting church right in its process, really does release people into ministry. So we had a lot of people busy out there doing what God called them to do.

Mel: You started with 17 people and began to release them into ministry from day one. Those who stayed began immediately to get involved. How did that take shape?

Rick: We didn't have any money so everybody had to have a job. It was all about the ministry. We had more jobs than people—mowing, cleaning, bookkeeping, and everything that needs to be done in church and by the church—so everyone had to do something.

Another important thing was we realized we were not able to reach what I call the "professional Christian" because we couldn't compete. People who already attended church and were just looking for a new location probably were not going to find what they wanted with us. We didn't have all the stuff that the really successful congregations had in place. The only people we could reach were the lost because they didn't have an expectation of what a church was supposed to be. They just needed Jesus, so our people began to win souls. We focused on individuals who were not Christians.

When you make the focus and keep it on lost people, never the people already there, it keeps you healthy. Since our people concentrated on being the church not trying to control it, we continued to multiply, and leadership stayed with God-called leaders.

Three years before becoming a sovereign church, we established three positions for deacons. Their purpose was not to be leaders but workers at a different level. It already was in their spiritual DNA through our ongoing training. They just took more responsibility for the work load, and the church did even better because that was their reason for being elected, not to be power jockeys.

Years later, the church still is doing well. The pastor is doing an incredible job and he's handled everything well. The church continues to operate with basically the same men who had been on the board, rotating off and on, and they're still 100 percent behind him. He is allowed to lead.

Mel: When you resigned as pastor, you didn't just walk away and leave the church to muddle through, how did you help with the transition to keep the church on track?

Rick: We followed a process to expedite and simplify the pastoral transition. When it came time to leave, I did a seven-week "Goodbye Series." I dealt with who has control, who has authority, and who has responsibility in such times. We made it clear, one more time, the ministry belongs to the people but there are authorities in the church. In symbolism, I wore a mantle the last day and I hung it over what had been the pastor's chair. (In those days we had a pastor's chair on the platform). I reminded them that this mantle doesn't belong to anyone until God's man comes and accepts it.

After the new pastor was elected, I came back for a Sunday service and put the mantle on him to establish that he is now the spiritual authority in the house. On my final day as pastor, I also put certain mantles on the deacons and other mantles on the ministry staff members. This was to remind that those who are anointed for ministry of the Word operate in a different way than those anointed for the work of deacon. We established that they all would work together to keep the church healthy until the new leader came and then would give him full support. All this helped keep the priorities and the process clear for everyone before, during and after the transition.

Appendix 2
Tenure of Office

An issue closely related to when the people should vote is tenure of office. How long should the term be for a pastor? How long should deacons serve? The Bible does not address these and related questions, but the biblical flow of authority and the respective roles of the ministry officers support the practical insights offered in this section. Healthy churches are proving these principles work. Unhealthy churches are proving how badly they are needed.

Many congregations need to change their thinking on pastor tenure. They cultivate frequent turnovers with their short term limits and reelection requirements. Their purpose should be to find and keep God's choice as shepherd. The initial term of office should be long enough to allow him to prove his love and begin to implement the vision God has given. We have told pastors it will take several years to solidify their position in the hearts of the people.[52] Their first term has to be long enough to allow it. Subsequent terms should be longer. A revolving door for the parsonage suggests God's will is not the church's priority.

On the other hand, many pastors need to change their philosophy of ministry if it does not call for long term commitment. The man or woman of God should approach every assignment with an expectation or, at least, willingness to stay there for a lifetime. Pastors with two to three year patterns of longevity do not have the accumulated total of their ministry years as real experience. They have two or three years of experience repeated.

Sometimes it shows. When they cycle to the end of their typical tenure, they also reach the end of their outlines and developed resources. It is easy then to begin to think God may be leading them elsewhere. Pastor, resist the temptation until you know God, not expediency, is speaking. Seek God for new and relevant insights, His voice for your people today. It continuously will be your best material and, if God does send you somewhere else, it will be the first you want to share.

The Bible gives no guideline for how long deacons should serve. The two tracked after their selection in Acts 6, Stephen and Philip, soon moved on to become evangelists,[53] miracle-workers,[54] and, in the case of Stephen, a martyr.[55] There is a job not many would rush to fill.

The Acts accounts demonstrate the limitless potential of God-called servants. God can do anything He wants with a person full of faith and the Holy Spirit, but the experiences of Stephen and Philip do not suggest how long an individual should be a deacon. As a practical, healthy church mechanism, it is wise to have a rotation on the church board.

Deacons are called and gifted for service and that needs to be evident. They can be fruitful for a lifetime, but caution is in order that no individual take ownership of the position. There is no divine right for deacon, and even godly individuals entrenched become a problem rather than an answer for the church.

The constitution and bylaws of every church need to require deacons periodically to sit out of office for a specified time. The most common pattern seems to be two three-year terms then a rotation off the board for at least one year. A full term out of office probably would be better but may not be practical in smaller congregations. Whatever the length, there needs to be a specified time and distance with provision for someone else to come onto the board.

Some churches have implemented a system which rotates oversight of finances but allows deacons to continue serving without interruption. They have a 12-member deacon board but a three-person official board which deals with church finances and administrative matters. Deacons in this system may serve indefinitely, doing the work of deacons but not dealing with money matters or setting salaries.

The deacons select from their ranks the three members of the official board. These three may not succeed themselves. The official board rotates membership in order to stay fresh and to assure that no individual maintains control of church finances.

These practical measures all are designed to allow good deacons to fulfill their ministries without holding the purse strings too long. A healthy system will keep them in ministry not money.

NOTES

[1] Ephesians 4:12 (NASB)
[2] Matthew 16:18
[3] Romans 12:4-8
[4] 1 Corinthians 12:4-6
[5] John 4:26
[6] John 4:29
[7] John 21:22,23
[8] Mark 2:5-12
[9] 1 Peter 2:5-9
[10] Acts 17:6 (KJV)
[11] Ephesians 4:7-13
[12] Luke 6:13-16; Acts 1:26; Galatians 1:1, 15-17; 2:8
[13] Elwell, Walter. "Entry for 'Apostle."*Evangelical Dictionary of Theology*. Grand Rapids: Baker. 2001.
[14] 1 Timothy 1:2 and Titus 1:4
[15] "New Life Church Bylaws." New Life Church. May 13, 2008`. New Life Church, Web. 19 Nov 2009. <http://www.newlifechurch.org/pages.jsp?id=14>.

A group of Overseers will be selected for the purpose of providing support and outside accountability to both the Senior Pastor and the Board of Elders and for Dispute Resolution. They will provide spiritual guidance when necessary and will function as Overseers as described in Scripture to the body of New life Church. There will typically be three to five Overseers, they will be pastors of other churches, and will be nominated by the Senior Pastor and confirmed by a two thirds (2/3) vote of the Board of Elders. Should the Senior Pastor be disqualified for ministry, the Board of Elder will determine the role of the Overseers in the restoration process of the Senior Pastor. The Overseer must confirm the Board of Elders choice for a new Senior

Pastor by a two thirds (2/3) vote. The Overseers will have no other legal or fiscal authority over the Corporation. Overseers can be removed from office upon either a two thirds (2/3) vote of all the Overseers or upon a two thirds (2/3) vote of all the elders.

[12] Haggard, Ted. "Healing Overview." Ted Haggard. 04 Apr 2009. Web. 7 Nov 2009. <http://tedhaggard.com/overview.htm>.

[17] Acts 20:28-29

[18] 1 Peter 5:1-4

[19] Mark 3:27

[20] 1 Timothy 3:6-8

[21] Jamison, Robert, A.R. Fausset, and David Brown. "Acts 6:1-7." Commentary: Critical, Experimental, and Practical on the Old and New Testaments 1871. Web. 14 Nov 2009. <http://www.biblestudytools.com/commentaries/jamieson-fausset-brown/acts/acts-6.html>.

[22] I Timothy 3:13

[23] Matthew 28:18

[24] Matthew 8:8-10

[25] Acts 2:14-39, [authors' paraphrase]

[26] Mark 5:30

[27] Dr. Earl Creps, *The Holy Spirit in a Postmodern Generation,* North Texas Assemblies of God 23-Hour Seminar, October, 2003,

[28] 1 Timothy 5:22

[29] *Poole, Matthew. "1 Timothy 3." Matthew Poole's Commentary on the Holy Bible. WORDsearch Electronic Database. CD. 14 Nov 2009.*

[30] 2 Timothy 2:15

[31] Psalms 145:4 (ESV)

[32] John 21:21-23

[33] *Position Paper on Apostles and Prophets.* General Council of

the Assemblies of God. *.August 6, 2001. Web 7 Nov* 2009.
http://www.ag.org/top/beliefs/topic_index.cfm

[34] Poole, Matthew. "1 Timothy 2." Matthew Poole's
Commentary on the Holy Bible. WORDsearch Electronic
Database. CD. 14 Nov 2009.

[35] Matthew 18:17

[36] Exodus 17:11,12

[37] "IRS Training Materials - Governance."
IRS.gov Charities and Non-Profits. 23 Jul 2009. Web. 14 Nov.
2009.*Organizations*

[38] Acts 15:36-41

[39] 2 Timothy 4:11

[40] 1 Timothy 5:17

[41] Clark, Adam. "1 Timothy 5:17." Adam Clarke
Commentary: A Commentary and Critical Notes 1826.
WORDsearch Electronic Database. CD. 14 Nov 2009.

[42] Acts 5:1-11

[43] Acts 1:20-22

[44] Acts 6:3

[45] Acts 6:3

[46] Genesis 17:4,5

[47] James 2:23

[48] Genesis 14:17-20

[49] Acts 20:27

[50] 2 Timothy 2:15

[51] Garrison, Alton. *The 360-Degree Disciple,* North Texas District
Assemblies of God Ministers Retreat. Crowne Plaza Hotel
Riverwalk, San Antonio, Texas. 20 Oct. 2009. Address.

[52] *The Church that Works*, p. 98

[53] Acts 8:4; 21:8

[54] Acts 6:8; 8:4

[55] Acts 7:54-59